Drop shipping on Walmart for Beginners in 2024

Emy Diamondz

Copyright

The content contained in this book may not be reproduced, duplicated or transmitted without direct written permission from the author or the publisher.

Under no circumstances will any blame or legal responsibility be held against the publisher or author, for any damages, reparation or monetary loss due to the information contained within this book, either directly or indirectly.

Table of Contents

Introduction to Walmart

Walmart is one of the world's largest multinational retail corporations, known for its extensive chain of hypermarkets, discount department stores, and grocery stores. Founded by Sam Walton in 1962 in Rogers, Arkansas, Walmart has grown into a global retail powerhouse with a presence in over 25 countries and territories.

History

Walmart's journey began with a single store in Rogers, Arkansas, under the name "Walton's Five and Dime." Sam

Walton's vision was to provide customers with high-quality products at low prices, along with exceptional customer service. This focus on value and affordability laid the foundation for Walmart's success and rapid expansion.

In 1969, the company was incorporated as Walmart Inc., and by the 1970s, it had expanded beyond Arkansas, opening stores in neighboring states.

Throughout the 1980s and 1990s, Walmart experienced exponential growth, fueled by aggressive expansion, strategic acquisitions, and innovations in supply chain management.

Business Model

Walmart's business model revolves around offering a wide range of products at everyday low prices, catering to diverse customer needs and preferences.

The company operates various store formats, including Supercenters, discount stores, neighborhood markets, and Sam's Club warehouses.

Key elements of Walmart's business model include:

1. Everyday Low Prices: Walmart's commitment to offering low prices on a wide assortment of products attracts budget-conscious consumers and fosters customer loyalty.

2. Efficient Supply Chain: Walmart's sophisticated supply chain and inventory management systems enable the company to optimize logistics, minimize costs, and maintain

high levels of product availability.

3. Customer-Centric Approach: Walmart places a strong emphasis on customer satisfaction, with initiatives such as hassle-free returns, price matching, and convenient shopping experiences.

4. E-commerce and Omnichannel Presence: In recent years, Walmart has invested heavily in e-commerce and omnichannel initiatives to compete effectively

in the digital age. The company offers online shopping, grocery delivery, curbside pickup, and other convenient services to meet evolving consumer preferences.

Corporate Social Responsibility

Walmart is committed to corporate social responsibility (CSR) and sustainability initiatives aimed at addressing social, environmental, and economic challenges. The company focuses on areas such as environmental sustainability, diversity and inclusion, community engagement, and ethical sourcing practices.

As a global retail leader, Walmart continues to innovate and evolve to meet the needs of customers in an ever-changing retail landscape. With its focus on value, convenience, and sustainability, Walmart remains a dominant force in the retail industry, shaping the way people shop and live around the world.

Chapter 1: Understanding Dropshipping

Dropshipping has become a popular business model for entrepreneurs looking to start an online retail venture without the need for significant upfront investment in inventory.

In this chapter, we'll delve into the fundamentals of dropshipping, its advantages and disadvantages, and how it operates specifically on the Walmart platform.

What is Dropshipping?

Dropshipping is a retail fulfillment method where a store doesn't keep the products it sells in stock. Instead, when a store sells a product, it purchases the item from a third party and has it shipped directly to the customer. This means the seller doesn't have to handle the product directly or hold inventory.

Pros and Cons of Dropshipping

Pros:

1. Low Startup Costs: Dropshipping eliminates the need for inventory,

warehousing, and upfront product purchases, significantly reducing initial investment requirements.

2. Easy to Get Started: Setting up a dropshipping business is relatively straightforward, especially with platforms like Walmart, which provide infrastructure for sellers.

3. Flexibility: Since you don't have to manage inventory, you can easily add or remove products from your store without much

hassle.

4. Location Independence: Dropshipping can be managed from anywhere with an internet connection, offering freedom and flexibility in terms of location.

5. Wide Product Selection: With dropshipping, you can offer a wide variety of products without the constraints of physical storage space.

Cons:

1. Lower Profit Margins: Since you're not buying products in bulk, unit costs can be higher, leading to lower profit margins compared to traditional retail models.

2. Limited Control Over Inventory and Shipping: Relying on third-party suppliers means you have less control over inventory levels, product quality, and shipping times.

3. Supplier Dependence: Your business is reliant on the reliability and quality of your suppliers. If they fail to fulfill orders or provide subpar products, it reflects poorly on your brand.

4. Increased Competition: The barrier to entry in dropshipping is low, leading to a crowded marketplace and increased competition.

5. Complexities in Customer Service: Dealing with customer inquiries, returns, and complaints can be challenging when you're not directly handling the products.

How Dropshipping Works on Walmart
Walmart has established itself as a major player in the e-commerce space, providing opportunities for third-party sellers to leverage its platform through the Walmart Marketplace.

To start dropshipping on Walmart, sellers need to apply and be approved as Marketplace partners.

Once approved, sellers can list their products on Walmart's website, set their prices, and manage their inventory. When a customer places an order, Walmart notifies the seller, who then coordinates with their suppliers to fulfill the order and ship it directly to the customer.

Walmart provides sellers with tools and resources to manage their stores effectively, including analytics dashboards, customer support, and marketing opportunities. However, sellers must adhere to Walmart's policies and standards to maintain a positive reputation on the platform.

Understanding the dynamics of dropshipping, its advantages, and challenges is crucial for anyone looking to embark on this business model, especially on a platform as prominent as Walmart. By mastering these fundamentals, entrepreneurs can position themselves for success in the competitive world of e-commerce.

Chapter 2: Setting Up Your Business

Setting up your dropshipping business is an exciting venture that requires careful planning, research, and execution.

In this comprehensive guide, we'll walk you through the step-by-step process of establishing your business on the Walmart platform, from creating a seller account to selecting profitable products and finding reliable suppliers.

1. **Creating a Walmart Seller Account**

To get started with dropshipping on Walmart, you'll need to create a seller account on the Walmart Marketplace. Here's how to do it:

1. Visit Walmart Marketplace: Go to the Walmart Marketplace website and click on the "Apply Now" button to begin the application process.
2. Provide Information: You'll be asked to provide basic information about your

business, such as your company name, address, tax identification number, and contact details.

3. Complete Registration: Follow the prompts to complete your registration and agree to Walmart's terms and policies.

4. Wait for Approval: Once you've submitted your application, Walmart will review it and notify you of their decision via email. Approval times can vary, so be patient during this process.

5. Set Up Your Account: Upon approval, log in to your seller account and complete your profile, including adding payment information and setting up shipping preferences.

2. Choosing a Niche or Product to Sell:

Selecting the right niche or product is crucial for the success of your dropshipping business.

Here are some tips for choosing a profitable niche:

1. Research Market Trends: Use tools like Google Trends, Amazon Best Sellers, and social media to identify popular product categories and trends.

2. Evaluate Competition: Assess the level of competition within your chosen niche to determine if there's room for your business to thrive.

3. Consider Profit Margins: Look for products with healthy profit

margins to ensure that your business remains sustainable.

4. Think Long-Term: Choose a niche that you're passionate about and that has the potential for long-term growth and sustainability.

3. Finding Reliable Suppliers for Dropshipping:

Finding reliable suppliers is essential for ensuring product quality and timely order fulfillment. Here are some strategies for finding reputable suppliers:

1. Use Supplier Directories: Explore online directories like Alibaba, SaleHoo, and Worldwide Brands to find verified suppliers in your chosen niche.

2. Contact Manufacturers: Reach out directly to manufacturers of the products you want to sell to inquire about dropshipping arrangements.

3. Attend Trade Shows: Attend industry trade shows and conferences to connect with

potential suppliers and establish relationships face-to-face.

4. Check Reviews and Ratings: Look for suppliers with positive reviews and ratings from other dropshippers to ensure reliability and quality.

5. Request Samples: Before committing to a supplier, request samples of their products to evaluate quality firsthand.

By following these steps, you can lay the foundation for a successful dropshipping business on the Walmart platform. Remember to stay informed about market trends, continuously optimize your product offerings, and provide excellent customer service to drive growth and profitability.

Chapter 3: Optimizing Your Walmart Store

Optimizing your Walmart store is essential for attracting customers, driving sales, and building a successful dropshipping business.

In this chapter, we'll explore key strategies for designing an attractive storefront, writing compelling product descriptions, and implementing effective inventory and pricing strategies.

Designing an Attractive Storefront

Your storefront serves as the first point of contact for potential customers, so it's crucial to make a positive impression. Here are some tips for designing an attractive storefront on Walmart:

1. Choose a Professional Theme: Select a clean and professional theme for your store that reflects your brand identity and appeals to your target audience.

2. Use High-Quality Images: Use

high-resolution images that showcase your products in their best light. Include multiple angles and close-ups to give customers a clear view of what they're purchasing.

3. Optimize for Mobile: Ensure that your storefront is optimized for mobile devices, as a growing number of shoppers are using smartphones and tablets to browse and make purchases.

4. Highlight Top Sellers: Showcase your best-selling products

prominently on your storefront to grab the attention of visitors and encourage them to explore further.

5. Include Customer Reviews: Display customer reviews and testimonials to build trust and credibility with potential buyers. Positive reviews can help reassure customers and influence their purchasing decisions.

Writing Compelling Product Descriptions

Effective product descriptions are crucial for converting visitors into customers. Here's how to write compelling product descriptions that drive sales:

1. Focus on Benefits: Highlight the benefits and features of your products, emphasizing how they can solve problems or improve the lives of your customers.

2. Be Descriptive: Use descriptive language to paint a vivid picture

of the product and its uses. Provide details such as size, dimensions, materials, and specifications to help customers make informed decisions.

3. Address Pain Points: Identify the pain points or challenges that your target audience faces, and explain how your product can address those needs.

4. Use Persuasive Language: Use persuasive language to encourage action, such as "limited time offer" or "free

shipping on orders over $50."
Create a sense of urgency to
motivate customers to make a
purchase.

5. Optimize for SEO: Incorporate
   relevant keywords into your
   product descriptions to improve
   visibility and search engine
   rankings. Use keywords
   naturally and avoid keyword
   stuffing.

Managing Inventory and Pricing Strategies

Effective inventory and pricing strategies are essential for maximizing profits and maintaining customer satisfaction. Here's how to manage inventory and pricing effectively on Walmart:

1. Monitor Stock Levels: Keep a close eye on your inventory levels and restock products in a timely manner to avoid stockouts and backorders.

2. Set Competitive Prices: Research competitors' prices and adjust your pricing strategy accordingly to remain competitive. Consider factors such as product quality, shipping costs, and customer demand when setting prices.

3. Offer Discounts and Promotions: Run promotions, discounts, and special offers to incentivize purchases and attract customers. Consider offering

bundle deals, free gifts, or limited-time discounts to drive sales.

4. Implement Dynamic Pricing: Use dynamic pricing tools to adjust prices in real-time based on factors such as demand, competition, and inventory levels. This can help maximize profits and optimize pricing strategies.

5. Track Performance Metrics: Monitor key performance metrics such as sales, conversion

rates, and profit margins to evaluate the effectiveness of your pricing strategy and make adjustments as needed.

By optimizing your Walmart store with an attractive design, compelling product descriptions, and effective inventory and pricing strategies, you can enhance the shopping experience for customers and drive sales growth for your dropshipping business.

Chapter 4: Marketing and Sales Strategies

Effective marketing and sales strategies are essential for driving traffic to your Walmart store and converting visitors into customers.

In this chapter, we'll explore three key strategies: utilizing social media marketing, implementing SEO techniques, and leveraging paid advertising on Walmart and other platforms.

Utilizing Social Media Marketing

Social media platforms offer a

powerful way to connect with your target audience, build brand awareness, and drive traffic to your Walmart store. Here's how to utilize social media marketing effectively:

1. Identify Your Target Audience: Understand who your target audience is and which social media platforms they frequent. Focus your efforts on platforms where your audience is most active.

2. Create Engaging Content: Develop engaging content that

resonates with your audience and aligns with your brand identity. Use a mix of product photos, videos, customer testimonials, and behind-the-scenes content to keep followers engaged.

3. Engage with Your Audience: Actively engage with your audience by responding to comments, messages, and mentions. Foster a sense of community by encouraging user-generated content and

sharing customer stories.

4. Run Contests and Giveaways: Host contests, giveaways, and promotions to incentivize engagement and attract new followers. Encourage participants to share your content and tag friends to expand your reach.

5. Collaborate with Influencers: Partner with influencers and content creators in your niche to reach a larger audience and build credibility. Choose

influencers whose values align with your brand and whose followers match your target demographic.

Implementing SEO Techniques

Search engine optimization (SEO) plays a critical role in improving your Walmart store's visibility in search engine results and driving organic traffic.

Here are some SEO techniques to implement:

1. Optimize Product Titles and Descriptions: Use relevant keywords in your product titles and descriptions to improve visibility in search results. Focus on long-tail keywords that are specific to your products and have lower competition.

2. Optimize Images: Optimize product images by using descriptive filenames and alt tags that include keywords. This

helps search engines understand the content of the images and improve your store's overall SEO.

3. Create High-Quality Content: Publish high-quality blog posts, guides, and tutorials related to your products or niche. Content marketing not only helps improve your store's SEO but also establishes your expertise and authority in the industry.

4. Build Backlinks: Earn backlinks from reputable websites in your

industry to improve your store's authority and credibility.

5. Focus on quality over quantity and avoid spammy link-building tactics.

6. Optimize for Local SEO: If you have a physical storefront or offer local services, optimize your store for local SEO by including location-specific keywords and creating a Google My Business profile.

Leveraging Paid Advertising on Walmart and Other Platforms

Paid advertising can help you reach a larger audience, drive targeted traffic to your Walmart store, and increase sales. Here's how to leverage paid advertising effectively:

1. Walmart Sponsored Products: Take advantage of Walmart's Sponsored Products advertising platform to promote your products to shoppers actively

searching for related items on Walmart.com. Use targeted keywords and compelling ad copy to maximize your ad's effectiveness.

2. Social Media Advertising: Run paid advertising campaigns on social media platforms like Facebook, Instagram, and Pinterest to reach your target audience and drive traffic to your Walmart store. Use demographic targeting, retargeting, and lookalike

audiences to refine your targeting and maximize ROI.

3. Google Ads: Use Google Ads to target shoppers searching for products similar to yours on Google's search engine and display network. Create keyword-targeted search ads, display ads, and shopping ads to increase visibility and drive qualified traffic to your store.

4. Retargeting Campaigns: Implement retargeting campaigns to re-engage visitors

who have previously visited your store but didn't make a purchase. Serve targeted ads to these users across various platforms to encourage them to return and complete their purchase.

5. Track and Analyze Performance: Monitor the performance of your advertising campaigns closely and analyze key metrics such as click-through rates, conversion rates, and return on ad spend (ROAS).

Use this data to optimize your campaigns and allocate your advertising budget effectively.

By utilizing social media marketing, implementing SEO techniques, and leveraging paid advertising on Walmart and other platforms, you can effectively promote your Walmart store, drive targeted traffic, and increase sales. Continuously monitor and refine your marketing strategies to stay competitive and adapt to evolving consumer behavior and market trends.

Chapter 5: Managing Operations and Scaling

Managing operations and scaling your dropshipping business are crucial aspects of long-term success.

In this comprehensive guide, we'll explore strategies for handling customer service and returns, analyzing data to improve performance, and scaling your dropshipping business effectively.

Handling Customer Service and

Returns

Providing excellent customer service is essential for building trust and loyalty with your customers. Here's how to effectively handle customer service and returns:

1. Prompt Communication: Respond to customer inquiries, messages, and complaints promptly and professionally. Aim to provide timely solutions to any issues or concerns raised by customers.

2. Clear Policies: Clearly

communicate your return, refund, and exchange policies to customers to set expectations and avoid misunderstandings. Make sure your policies are easily accessible on your website or store.

3. Streamlined Returns Process: Implement a streamlined returns process to make it easy for customers to return products if they're not satisfied. Provide clear instructions and prepaid return labels to facilitate the

return process.

4. Handle Complaints with Empathy: When dealing with customer complaints or issues, approach them with empathy and understanding. Apologize for any inconvenience caused and work towards finding a satisfactory resolution for the customer.

5. Learn from Feedback: Use customer feedback and reviews as valuable insights to identify areas for improvement and

make necessary adjustments to your products or services.

Analyzing Data to Improve Performance

Data analysis is essential for identifying trends, optimizing strategies, and making informed decisions to improve your business's performance. Here's how to analyze data effectively:

1. Track Key Metrics: Monitor key performance metrics such as sales, conversion rates, average

order value, and customer acquisition cost. Use analytics tools like Google Analytics or Walmart's seller dashboard to track and analyze these metrics.

2. Identify Patterns and Trends: Analyze sales data to identify patterns and trends in customer behavior, product performance, and market demand. Use this information to make data-driven decisions about product selection, pricing, and marketing strategies.

3. Segment Your Audience: Segment your customer base based on demographics, purchasing behavior, and other relevant criteria. This allows you to personalize marketing messages, tailor product recommendations, and optimize customer experience.

4. A/B Testing: Conduct A/B tests to experiment with different variables such as product descriptions, pricing strategies, and marketing campaigns.

Analyze the results to determine which approach yields the best outcomes and refine your strategies accordingly.

5. Forecasting and Planning: Use historical data and trend analysis to forecast future sales and inventory needs. This helps you plan ahead and avoid stockouts or overstocking, optimizing inventory management and cash flow.

Scaling Your Dropshipping Business for Long-Term Success

Scaling your dropshipping business involves expanding operations, increasing sales, and maximizing profitability over time. Here's how to scale your business effectively:

1. Automate Processes: Implement automation tools and software to streamline repetitive tasks such as order processing, inventory management, and customer communication. This frees up time and resources to focus on strategic growth initiatives.

2. Diversify Product Offerings: Expand your product catalog by adding new products or expanding into complementary niches. Diversifying your offerings can attract new customers and increase sales opportunities.

3. Optimize Supply Chain: Strengthen relationships with reliable suppliers and optimize your supply chain to ensure timely order fulfillment and consistent product quality.

Consider working with multiple suppliers to mitigate risks and ensure continuity of supply.

4. Invest in Marketing: Allocate resources towards marketing and advertising initiatives to increase brand visibility, attract new customers, and drive sales. Experiment with different marketing channels and strategies to identify what works best for your business.

5. Monitor Cash Flow: Keep a close eye on your cash flow and

financial metrics to ensure your business remains financially healthy and sustainable during periods of growth. Invest profits back into the business strategically to fuel further expansion.

By effectively managing operations, analyzing data to improve performance, and scaling your dropshipping business for long-term success, you can build a thriving and profitable enterprise that stands the test of time. Stay agile, adapt to changing market dynamics, and continuously innovate to maintain a competitive edge in the e-commerce landscape.

Conclusion

In conclusion, establishing and running a successful dropshipping business on platforms like Walmart requires careful planning, diligent execution, and continuous optimization. Throughout this guide, we've explored the key components of building and scaling a dropshipping venture, from setting up your business on Walmart to managing operations, analyzing data, and scaling for long-term success.

By understanding the fundamentals of dropshipping, entrepreneurs can leverage its advantages while mitigating its challenges. From selecting profitable niches to finding reliable suppliers and optimizing product listings, every aspect of the dropshipping process plays a critical role in driving sales and profitability.

Furthermore, effective marketing and sales strategies, such as social media marketing, SEO techniques, and paid advertising, are essential for attracting customers and increasing brand visibility in a competitive marketplace. Additionally, providing exceptional customer service and analyzing data to make informed decisions are key factors in building trust with customers and optimizing business performance.

Ultimately, scaling a dropshipping business requires a combination of strategic planning, operational efficiency, and continuous innovation. By staying agile, adapting to market trends, and prioritizing customer satisfaction, entrepreneurs can position their businesses for sustainable growth and long-term success in the dynamic world of e-commerce.

With dedication, perseverance, and a focus on delivering value, the possibilities for success in dropshipping are limitless.

9 798888 767875